High Praise for Dr. Rick Voyles

"Dr. Rick Voyles is an exceptional ADR (Alternative Dispute Practitioner) practitioner whose deep understanding of human nature has formed his multi-disciplinary approach to conflict resolution. As a teacher, he has always incorporated new ideas being one of the first in the field to demonstrate in everyday life situations how factors such as religion, gender, culture and emotion influence conflict. In his latest contribution to the field, Rick provides insights, tools and techniques for decoding conflict. Throughout the text, the conversational tone invites the reader to think through the assumptions we make about conflict and how we can understand things differently. This approach is so important in demystifying how conflicts are resolved and inviting a more constructive dialogue on how we can improve human relationships."

–Deborah S. Laufer
Director, Federal ADR Network–

"Understanding Conflict: What We Are Fighting For? is an elegant introduction to how to manage conflict, not avoid it. The usual presentation is that "the other person is the problem" or that "there is only one solution." But Voyles shows that "solution is not the same as resolution." The latter requires finding the "positive request" buried in the complaint, distinguishing what one wants from what one really needs, and learning that establishing "the truth (about the past) does not resolve conflicts." These hard lessons are clearly laid out and illustrated by cases. Also, each chapter very helpfully ends with a worksheet showing how to apply the lessons taught. This book is a must for those who want to manage and resolve conflict."

–R. David Blumenthal,
Jay and Leslie Cohen
Professor of Judaic Studies, Emory University–

"Just because we all speak the same language does not mean we know how to talk to each other. It is a natural desire to be understood; however clear communication is a talent possessed by few, leaving most of us floundering in a sea of misunderstandings and hurt feelings. This book is useful not only for professionals who manage people for a living, but for anyone wanting more joy out of life."

–Debbie Unterman, Hypnotherapy Trainer,
Author, Talking to My Selves: Learning to
Love the Voices in Your Head –

"Conflict is misunderstood." Thus begins Dr. Rick Voyles' book *Understanding Conflict,* and it is an undeniably powerful truth. Except that Dr. Voyles does understand conflict, and he explains the nature of it and, importantly, how to address conflict to enhance relationships, as well as anyone in the field. This is no surprise, for Dr. Voyles is the best live educator from whom I have ever learned. This book, based on his lectures, is a brilliant articulation of the benefit – yes, benefit! – of addressing conflict and of the manner in which to get what you need when doing so. This book is a gift, and I recommend it to those who seek more value, more insight and even a degree of peace in their relationships and in their lives."

–Martin L. Ellin
Executive Director
Atlanta Volunteer Lawyers Foundation–

"In this important book, Rick Voyles shows us how we can see conflict in a new light—as an opportunity for building relationships, even intimacy. Individuals, couples, and communities will all benefit from the knowledge, techniques and skills this book offers in a very accessible format. Learn how to fight fair with everybody winning!"

–Lanny Peters, Pastor,
Oakhurst Baptist Church–

Dr. Rick Voyles

"The Conflict Doctor"™

Donna,

May all your conflicts be good.

Rick

Understanding

Conflict

What are We

Fighting For?

Published by White Feather Press.
(www.whitefeatherpress.com)

ISBN 978-0-9822487-1-3

Printed in the United States of America

Exterior cover photo ©iStockphoto.com/David Cerven

Author photo courtesy of Kristie Voyles

White Feather Press

Making the world a better place
One reader at a time

Table of Contents

Acknowledgements

No accomplishment is the result of one person's effort. This book is no exception. I want to express immense gratitude to Skip and Sara Coryell at White Feather Press for seeing something of value in these pages and being willing to take a risk on me.

I would like to tip my hat in appreciation to every teacher that taught me, every book I've read and every conflict I have had. Of course some in this list are more notable than others and bare special mention. My close friends and the good people at Oakhurst Baptist Church for the support they have given me through difficult times. My business partners at Conflict Resolution Academy, Carol Rice and Karen Walters for their support and hard work. I especially want to acknowledge Janet Fluker for being my best friend, for believing in me and for loving me.

Dedication

To my girls Kristie, Ashley and Rachel who have taught me more about life, love and relationship than all of my formal education put together. I love you and I am proud of you.

A Note from the Author

We all live in relationship. When our personal and professional relationships are not strong and healthy, our mental, emotional and physical health suffers too. All of us are in an important relationship somewhere, whether it be personal or professional. How are your important relationships going? Have you picked up this book, because one or more of your important relationships are causing you pain?

I have written this book in the hopes of helping you with your personal and professional relationships. I believe that conflict has within it a seed of positive potential that, when managed effectively, can create stronger teams in the workplace, can create healthy diversity in our communities and can create loving personal relationships. I offer to you here what conflict has taught me and present to you some of the skills and techniques that have changed my personal and professional relationships for the better. I hope they can do the same for you.

Dr. Rick Voyles

What You Can Expect to Get Out of This Book

We will look at:

- how conflict works
- how to recognize conflict communication
- how to manage a healthy venting process using effective communication skills
- how to explore and discover the needs behind your conflict
- how to get out of the past where people in conflict get stuck
- how to move into the future where all resolution lies
- four conflict management secrets most people don't know

Chapter One
Conflict is Misunderstood

Conflict is misunderstood. When you think of conflict, discomfort, anxiety, pain, frustration, fear, anger, grudge, arguing, shouting, abandonment, abuse and many more negative images come to mind.

However, growth, under-standing, teamwork, learning, trust, communication, coop-eration, harmony, strength,

> ... as a conflict-avoidant culture we are intimacy starved.

friendship, unity, awareness, success, progress, insight, and increased intimacy are some of the positive things that can also result from conflict. When I present this list, almost everyone expresses surprise that intimacy is on the list. Most people do not associate intimacy increase with conflict, when in fact you cannot have intimacy without conflict. It is no coincidence that as a conflict-avoidant culture we are intimacy starved.

Intimacy is the closeness nurtured within the gap between your differences. Without the differences, without the disagreements there can be no real intimacy. Being intimacy starved relates directly to our desire to keep conflict out of our life. It is not conflict in our life that is the problem, but an inability to manage the conflict that enters our life. Conflict is not the problem. Our lack of skill in managing conflict is the problem.

In fact, we spend more time and energy in our culture mastering conflict-avoidance skills than nurturing the conflict management skills that will produce the positive outcomes we

> **Conflict is not the problem. Our lack of skill in managing conflict is the problem.**

desire most. We teach our children not to fight. We teach them to share, sacrifice, give up and give in for the greater good. This can create a calm classroom, a stress-free work environment, a happy home. And that is good.

The problem is that often these kids grow up with only the skills of sharing, sacrificing, giving up and giving in as a response to conflict. They never learn skills for how to fight, when to fight, and deciding what's worth fighting for. When they come across something they are not willing to give in on or give up on, or share or sacrifice, they end up demonstrating their profound lack of skill. There are things worth fighting for. There is a time to fight and a time not to fight. And there are ways to fight while honoring personal and professional relationships.

Without conflict skills, we fail. We create harm, disrespect and damage and lose valued relationships. We perpetuate the negative outcomes of conflict, reinforcing our belief that conflict is something to avoid at all cost. So we redouble our resolve, increase our conflict-avoidant energies and continue to misunderstand conflict.

> There is a seed of positive potential at the center of all conflict.

Conflict can be positive. There is a seed of positive potential at the center of all conflict. In order to nurture this seed to flower, we must rethink our negative understanding of conflict. We must pay attention to how conflict works and bring to conflict those skills and techniques that reinforce its positive potential. This does not mean conflict will not be hard, nor does it mean conflict will never hurt; but if it is going to be hard and hurt anyway, then why not manage it in a way that maximizes the positive outcomes we desire the most. Let's begin by rethinking our misunderstanding of conflict.

— The Definition of Conflict —

A conflict results in any setting where there are incompatible goals, interests, feelings or principles. [1]

How many people does it take to have a conflict? It takes two to tango, but it only takes one to have a conflict. Has any of you ever been on a diet plan? Have you gone out to eat and everyone around you is ordering dishes you wish you could have? You find yourself regretting going to dinner. You consider looking for thinner friends, or maybe you should get fatter friends. You are in a conflict with yourself. You want to lose weight and you want that tasty dish. Who will win?

For me, it's exercising. I want to be healthier, to get into shape, but I also want to sleep in, watch TV, spend time with my granddaughter, see a movie with my daughter. All the things I want to do get in the way of my desire to be healthier. I am dissatisfied with the shape I am in, the profile I reflect in the mirror. I am in a conflict with myself.

When we think about conflict we think of two people arguing, but we also get into conflicts with circumstances, time and mechanical objects. I am sitting at the exit of a parking deck, a mechanical arm

> It takes two to tango, but it only takes one to have a conflict.

---

1   Capobianco, S., Davis, M., and Kraus, L. *Conflict Dynamics Profile*. St. Petersburg, FL. : Eckard College Leadership Development Institute, 1999.

hanging between me and my journey home for the evening. In a woman's voice (why do they decide to use a woman's voice?) the machine instructs me to pay "her" five dollars for my freedom. I do not want to pay for my freedom. My freedom has already been paid for; why should I have to pay for it again? Crashing the gate is a conflict-resolution technique. It would, in fact, end this conflict. It might create other conflicts, but so would paying this *"woman"* five dollars.

Incompatible feelings, principles, goals, interests will creep up in our personal and professional interactions. Which means almost anything can cause a conflict.

— Conflict is Inevitable —

You can no more live life without conflict than you can live life without oxygen. In all likelihood you will not be able to live the rest of this week without some encounter with incompatible goals, interests, feelings or principles. Not only is it inevitable, it is essential. You cannot experience change, partnership, growth, community, learn-

> Conflict is simply a request for communication.

ing, intimacy, effectiveness, success, improvement, insight (to name just a few) without conflict.

So why is it we do not get up every morning expectant

and excited about the conflict we might encounter today? Why do we not look for it, knowing it is out there, coming our way, understanding the life-giving potential it might provide today?

At a conference where I was speaking a woman blurted, "Oh, I wish you could just suck all the conflict out of my life." My immediate thought was, "Be careful what you ask for." She did not understand conflict and as a result was pleading for an outcome that most likely would create even more pain and loneliness in her life.

Conflict is simply a request for communication: nothing more. So why are we so fearful of a request for communication? You come home from work; you ask your spouse, *"How was your day?"* You get no response. Adjusting your body position to maximize eye content and suggest genuine interest, you try again. *"How was your day?"* In reply, you get a shrug, along with a soft grunt. What are the next words your spouse wants to hear out of your mouth?

"What's wrong, honey?"

How did your spouse communicate a desire to talk to you? By ignoring you and giving you the silent treatment. The reason I know this is a request for communication is that this delivery method only works with you in the room. Coming home one day and finding the closets and drawers empty and the car gone sends the message your spouse does not want to talk to you. Getting the shrug and the grunt is really a clear offer for communication.

> *"I'll tell you what's wrong! Why didn't you call me?"*

Strong antagonistic emotions and responses are evidence of valued issues and relationships. It takes a lot of energy to engage in a conflict. It is very hard to engage someone in an argument or to fight about something they care nothing about. Every conflict is evidence of an important issue or relationship.

> **Every conflict is evidence of an important issue or relationship.**

When my youngest daughter was 16, her mother and I argued over what time she should be home after being out with her friends. Mom argued her curfew should be 11:00 PM. I argued she should stay at home (away from boys) until she was 25 years of age!

The point of the story is not who won the argument. (That's not the point because I lost.) The point is, we both valued the same thing: Our daughter's safety. Each of us saw a different way to ensure her safety. We argued about something we cared about. We argued because we cared, which leads us to our first secret about conflict management.

Conflict Management Secret #1:
People only fight about things they care about.

When someone hires me to resolve their conflict, I come knowing one thing: the people engaging in this fight care about something. One of my jobs as an effective conflict manager is to figure out what it is they both care about.

> You argue as a couple because the relationship is important to you.

During my seminars I give out a homework assignment. Go home, find someone who says they love you and engage them in an argument. I get mixed reactions. Some laugh, saying, "That will be easy." Others, express worry. In fact, the assignment is "tongue-in-cheek;" I do not really want them to start a fight. But I am trying to make a point.

Because people tend to fight about issues or relationships of value to them, my point is this: If you cannot engage them in an argument, then you have either picked an issue they care nothing about, or you are in a relationship they care nothing about.

You argue as a couple because the relationship is important to you. All couples fight, all couples argue, because they care. When you stop caring, you will stop fighting. The problem is not the fighting or arguing. The problem is not knowing how to fight in a way that maximizes the seed of positive potential within every conflict. What if you could learn to fight (you are going to fight anyway because you care about many things) in such a way that your relationship could, in fact, grow as a result? Would such skill be of value to you?

— The Opposite of Love —

Most people assume the opposite of love is hate. It is not. Hate is an incredibly binding emotion. If you ever get the chance to work with divorcing couples, you can see the binding power of hate. It keeps divorcing couples enmeshed.

The opposite of love is not hate; it is indifference.[2] Indifference means this person could not care less about either your issue or your relationship.

> **The opposite of love is not hate; it is indifference.**

Indifference cannot maintain the energy necessary for conflict. Think of the times you chose not to engage in a debate or conflict simply because it was not worth the time or the energy to you.

Here is the scary part! If we will only learn to care less about enough things we will never be in a conflict again. In fact, no one would ever be in a conflict again if all of us

---

2   The insight was introduced to me by Elie Wiesel in the video *Weapons of the Spirit*, written, produced and directed by Pierre Sauvage, 1990.

would simply care less. Is that what peace looks like? It is if you define peace as the opposite of conflict. Let's not define peace that way! If conflict is inevitable and peace is possible, then the two must be able to coexist.

Conflict Management Secret #2:
You can only control two things: yourself and your attitude.

Many of us get into a conflict when we try to control someone else's behavior, attitude, thinking or feeling. We try to change them. When you try to control anything that is outside of your control, then you are the one out of control.

I see people throw out the window every morning the only two things they control. They decide to be grumpy or angry simply because it is cold or rainy outside. They let the weather decide who they are going to be today. Or they get upset and take it out on others because they got caught in traffic on the way to work. These people allow situations or circumstances to decide who they are, letting go of control of the only two things they have control over. The irony is, these same people make attempts then to control other

> Every conflict is an opportunity for you to demonstrate who you are.

people, how they act, and who they are.

Effective conflict management begins with you. You control who you are and how you behave, and nothing else. Every conflict is an opportunity for you to step forward with a demonstration of who you are. When I see people behave poorly, I think, "Your skills are showing," which is to say they are clearly demonstrating their complete lack of skills. Who will you be during your next conflict? With a little conflict understanding and a few skills, you could be the best "*you*" ever by pulling out the power of the positive potential within your next conflict.

> We should never fear conflict. It is a request for communication by someone who cares.

— Conclusion —

Conflict is not the evil-doer we think it is. Good, even great things can come out of conflict. We need to take the time to understand what conflict is before we will be able to work with conflict rather than working against it. When we learn to work with conflict, we are better able to nurture that seed of positive potential lying dormant inside our conflicts.

Conflict is inevitable. It is impossible to live our lives

without conflict. We should, in fact, stop trying. As simply a request for communication, we need not fear conflict. In fact, we should fear indifference. Conflict is evidence of caring and reveals for us the first secret most people do not know about conflict.

Always remember the secrets of conflict management:

Conflict Secret #1: People only fight about things they care about.

Conflict Secret #2: You can control only two things: yourself and your attitude.

When I try to control something outside of my control, then I am the one who is out of control.

If I am going to become an effective manager of my conflicts, then I must rethink how I look at conflict and learn a few skills that will work to resolve the inevitable conflict coming my way. This way I afford myself every opportunity to be the best me in all of my personal and professional relationships.

> When I try to control things outside of my control, then I am the one who is out of control.

Let's get to work. Now that we have a better perspective

on what conflict is, let's begin to look at how conflict works by looking at some of the dynamics of conflict communication.

— Understanding Conflict Worksheet —

I. People fight only over things they care about.

1) Think back to the last argument you had (either at work or at home). Think about what it was you were arguing for. List below what you were valuing:

2) Think back to the last argument you had (either at work or at home). Think about what it was the other person was arguing for. List below what you think they were valuing:

II. You can only control two things: yourself and your attitude (who you are and how you act).

1) Think back to the last argument you had (either at work or at home). Think about what you were arguing for. List below what you were trying to control:

2) Think back to the last argument you had (either at work or at home). Think about what you were arguing for. List below what you can control:

Personal Notes and Lessons Learned

CHAPTER TWO
Conflict Communication

Communication is hard. Once we are into the conflict, communication takes on greater complication. I often see three harmful communication dynamics occurring when people drop into conflict. Let's explore these three dynamics in order to better understand how conflict works.

Conflict Communication Dynamic #1: The Person Becomes the Problem

Let me explain this harmful dynamic by demonstrating how this sounded in my house. *"You are not listening to me."* This is an easy, common phrase between people in conflict. I, myself, used this phrase, before I developed some conflict-management skills and techniques.

This phrase can be delivered without yelling, without even a condescending tone. This phrase can be delivered simply as a matter of fact.

"You are not listening to me."

However, let me give you the full translation of this line so you can understand its powerful negative impact.

"You are not listening to me. If you were listening to me, then you would hear the clarity of my argument, feel the undeniable weight of my evidence and agree with me. You are not agreeing with me, so, therefore, you must not be listening to me."

The short version is simply:

"We would not be having this argument if you were not an idiot."

There it is. The other person is the problem. Obviously, if the other person would just give in, give up and agree, the conflict would be over. But nooooo...

> We would not be having this argument if you were not an idiot!

Now I have to engage in the work, energy and effort to show you where you are wrong. This energy is designed to change the other person: to change their thinking, feelings or behavior. Do you know how hard it is to change someone's mind, how they feel, or how they choose to act? If you have ever been in a conflict, you do.

I did not necessarily call anyone an "idiot." This was too

harsh, too confrontational. To call someone an idiot makes me a mean person. Name calling might make the other person walk away, and then I would not get the chance to present my thorough explanation of why they were wrong. Instead of name calling, I would say something like:

> *"Your conclusion does not follow from your premise."*
>
> *– or –*
>
> *"You have not incorporated all of the relevant facts into your argument."*
>
> *– or –*
>
> *"You have a tendency to be judgmental... (followed with the quick jab to the heart) ... like your mother."*

Even if someone had a good point, I could still make them the problem by saying something like: "Your point would be stronger if you stated it this way, or included this fact," so that I could undermine even good points by attacking the other person.

> **Without conflict skills, some people draw on an arsenal of verbal, emotional and psychological attacks.**

Without conflict skills, people end up drawing on an arsenal of "attack" tactics such as verbal attacks, emotional attacks and psychological attacks. Some people even go so far as physically attacking the person they perceive as the problem in the hopes of getting them to change. Fighting is an effort to change the other person; this happens when you make the other person the problem.

I tell people all the time, *"Violence is a conflict resolution technique. It may not always be the most effective technique, but it is still a resolution technique."* In my experience it is ineffective to tell children to never fight. This strategy promotes conflict avoidance, not conflict resolution. Instead of teaching people to never fight, I want to teach people not to make the other person the problem. I want to teach them skills for how to get around this typical conflict-communication dynamic. The way around making the other person the problem employs the technique of need exploration. By providing people with skills and techniques more effective than avoidance, we give them a choice. People will often choose the technique that gets them what they want.

> Teaching people to never fight promotes conflict avoidance, not conflict resolution.

Conflict Communication Dynamic #2: A Single Solution Mindset

Conflict is not the lack of a solution. Conflict is the result of people arguing over two different solutions. Conflict is never bereft of solutions. Most conflict managers believe conflict resolution is simply the task of finding a solution to the problem; figure out the problem and brainstorm a solution. This is unfortunately a serious problem-producing myth about conflict. What is needed in a conflict is not for someone to add another solution to the list, but for parties to get beyond their single-solution mindset. Consider the argument below:

"You are wrong and should admit it!"

"I am not! You just don't understand me."

Can you hear the solution? Can you hear the other person as the problem?

1st Translation: "You cannot see the facts."
(You're the problem.) And, "You are
stubborn."

2nd Translation: "I am right." And,
"You are too stupid to get me." (You're the
problem.)

In the first statement the solution is: Stop being stubborn. In the second statement the solution is: Understand me.

Nobody comes to a conflict without a solution in mind. Conflict exists because each has a solution the other cannot accept. They are in conflict over differing solutions. Each person believes they have a clear understanding of the situation and based upon their evaluation know exactly what would balance the scales of justice.

People get stuck on their solution. It is what we call in conflict management "their position". In my experience, it is hard for people to give up their position. Giving up their position suggests that the other person's position is right. To agree with the other person's solution, therefore, suggests that I and my position are wrong. People do not like to be wrong, "I may not be right, but I know I am not wrong."

A single-solution mindset is one of the things that get individuals stuck when entering into a conflict. The way around a single-solution mindset employs the technique of need exploration.

Everyone is very, very good at coming up with solutions, quick to describe a cause and outline a remedy for the conflict. Solutions do not resolve conflicts; need exploration and negotiation resolve conflicts. We are great problem solvers, but lousy need

> Overcome a single-solution mindset using need-exploration techniques.

explorers. When great problem solvers approach a conflict without doing need exploration, they often create more problems than the one they started with. Even good solutions without adequate and clear need exploration can be dissatisfying at best and insulting at worst.

I will get to the skill of need exploration in Chapter 4. We will need to spend a lot of time there if I am going to communicate the importance of this often overlooked skill in conflict management.

But before we go there, I need to tell you about the third conflict communication dynamic.

Conflict Communication Dynamic #3: An Imbalanced Personal State

We all live within a balanced personal state between our emotions and our intellect. Each is a source of data within our decision-making process. When we get into conflict, we tend to silence one of these data sources and to begin operating out of an imbalanced personal state.

I don't know who you are, which voice you silence within yourself, but I have a tendency to push out and silence my emo-

> We all live within a balanced personal state between our emotions and our intellect.

tional voice, overcompensating with my intellect. Anyone shocked? I didn't think so.

When I silence my emotional side I look and sound calm, cool and collected in the midst of the conflict. Looking at me and listening to me you would not necessarily believe I was even in a conflict, because my behavior does not fit the stereotype of what a conflict looks like: shouting or strong emotional outbursts.

However, by cutting off my emotional side I become numb to the nature of my connection with the other person in the conflict. I become cold and calculating, bent on revenge. I end up measuring the amount of the other person's suffering necessary for me to feel better about what they did to me. While I look and sound reasonable, in reality, inside, I am plotting your pain. I am hurt and I want you to hurt as much, if not more, than I am hurting. Only then will there be any rebalancing the scales of justice.

> By cutting off my emotional side I become numb to the nature of my connection with the other person.

When I am like this I sever the connection between us. I seek retribution at the expense of the relationship. The problem I always have when I do this is that when I feel better, when I am back in a balanced personal state, when the emotional voice is allowed back into my awareness, I want the connection to continue. I want the relationship to have been repaired after you have suffered my retaliation. Guess what. This response does not work and results in damaging my relationships.

The logic is faulty (as it always is when the intellect tyrannically suppresses the emotion's voice). The logic follows an authoritarian model of punishment and reward exemplified by the saying: "The beatings will continue until morale improves!" I wrongly worked out of the premise that if you suffer every time you hurt me then, like Pavlov's dog, you will make sure never to hurt me again in order not to suffer a severe shock for your behavior. Of course this strategy fails me. It is wrong on so many different levels, not the least of which is that it is an abuse of power and a serious boundary violation.

The other option available when operating from an imbalanced personal state is to suppress and silence the intellect, letting the emotional voice rule the day. This is often the stereotype we have of people in conflict. We picture people screaming and yelling at the top of their lungs, maybe throwing things or throwing themselves around the room. Every textbook I have read on conflict management admonishes people not to become emotional during conflict, that emotions are the catalyst for escalating conflict.

"Don't be so emotional."

"When you calm down and become reasonable, then we can continue this conversation."

The admonition implies, and almost stresses, turning off the emotions is a necessary component to successful conflict resolution. While this is somewhat true, it masks the danger of the tyranny of the intellect and reason.

The problem is not our emotions. The problem is our imbalance. The result I often see is the overrational criticizing the over emotional for being "emotional." Both are in an imbalanced personal state and a terrible position to effectively resolve this conflict. A solution offered out of an imbalanced personal state is in danger of generating resentment, distrust, manipulation, misuse of power and boundary violations. I do not want people making decisions from within an imbalanced personal state.

We tend to gender-stereotype this imbalance, seeing women as typically silencing the intellect and becoming emotional, seeing men as typically silencing the emotions and becoming very intellectual. While men have been rewarded more often in our culture for maintaining an imbalanced personal state, it is a bad assumption to go into a conflict expecting this stereotype. I have seen many women capable of being cold, calculating, bent on revenge, as well as many men who become emotionally driven during a conflict.

I cannot tell you the number of women in my seminars

> The problem is not our emotions. The problem is our imbalance.

who have found hope and affirmation from this concept of imbalance. Because of the stereotype, women often feel the brunt of the western bias for reason and intellect. They tell me stories of feeling they have to go along with the oppression of emotionality. They have been expected to participate in a resolution process they feel is one-sided and wrong.

> Both intellect and emotion are necessary to a healthy conflict resolution.

"You mean emotions are not a bad thing?" Yes! I mean emotions are not a bad thing. Emotions, even passionate, loud, intense emotions are not bad; and there are appropriate and inappropriate ways to communicate our emotions, even our intense, passionate, loud emotions. Emotion out of balance with the intellect is a bad thing. Intellect out of balance with the emotions is equally bad. Both are necessary to a healthy decision-making process, and, therefore, both are necessary to an effective resolution process.

— Getting Back the Balance —

If you rush the conflict management process, you risk people's making decisions in an imbalanced personal state. Then, when they calm down, get back into balance, begin seeing more clearly, they often resent and regret their decisions. The result is suspicion of the process used to resolve the conflict, as well as resentment for the outcome.

There are two techniques to address this conflict communication dynamic. The first technique is managing and maintaining a healthy venting process. The second technique is need exploration. These two can be effectively combined; but for training purposes, I will separate these two techniques here, looking at the venting process in Chapter 3 and addressing the technique of need exploration in Chapter 4.

> A healthy venting process allows me to restore connection to myself.

A healthy venting process allows a person to "let off steam" that builds up inside, silencing one of the two voices necessary for healthy decision-making. Think of a balloon. Inside the middle of this balloon is a flexible partition. Above the partition represents your emotional voice. Below the partition represents your intellectual voice. As long as the partition is in the middle you have balance and two healthy voices informing your decision-making. During conflict, pressure builds on one side or the other, depending upon who you are. As this pressure builds, the partition moves in the opposite direction, squeezing the space of one voice into a smaller and smaller portion, causing that voice to become weaker and quieter.

A healthy venting process is a connection restoration process. It allows me to restore connection to myself, restoring balance between my emotions and my intellect. The pressure is removed and the connection with myself (balance) and the one I am in conflict with is restored. In some cases, my connections can even intensify.

Venting will take two characteristically different forms. One will be what we stereotypically expect: emotional outburst. The other: over-intellectualizing. Either way, healthy venting is often necessary to allow a person to retrieve personal balance.

To allow someone to vent on you during a conflict is a masterful skill. It is not easy. We have to distinguish between healthy venting and verbal abuse, between healthy venting and boundary violation. I am not asking you to lie down and take it. I am asking you to employ the techniques of a skilled conflict manager in order to take this conflict in the direction of resolution. The techniques associated with healthy venting management are predominantly communication skills. Your goal will be to keep the door of communication open.

I will show you five communication techniques for keeping that communication door open in Chapter 3.

— **Conflict Communication Worksheet** —

I. The Person is the Problem

"You are not listening."

A great way to identify ways you make the other person the problem is to review the list of statements you made when venting on a friend about the person you are in a conflict with.

"She doesn't care about me."

"He never listens."

"He is lazy."

"He cares more about football than he does me."

"She is controlling."

"She suffocates me."

"My boss is a control freak."

"He doesn't carry his weight around here."

Think back to your last argument. Write comments you made or thought of making that cast the other person as the problem.

II. Single Solution Mindset

"You are wrong and should admit it!"

"I am not! You just don't understand me."

Can you hear the solution? Can you hear the other person as the problem?

Translation: "You cannot see the facts." (You're the problem.) And, "You are stubborn."
Solution: Stop being stubborn.

Translation: "I am right." And, "You are too stupid to get me." (You're the problem.)
Solution: Understand me.

Take the statements below and identify the solution:

1) "She doesn't care about me."

      Solution: Care about me.

2) "He never listens."

      Solution: _____

3) "He is lazy."

      Solution: _____

4) "He cares more about football, than he does me."

  Solution: _____

5) "She is controlling."

  Solution: _____

6) "She suffocates me."

  Solution: _____

7) "My boss is a control freak."

  Solution: _____

8) "He doesn't carry his weight around here."

  Solution: _____

III. Healthy Venting

1) Some of the ways I manage my healthy venting are to:

- Walk the dog.
- Watch TV.
- Go to a movie (alone or with a friend I want to vent on).
- Go to a coffee shop.
- Vent to a friend, asking them just to listen

(and not take to much stock of what I say).

- Write a letter (then destroy the letter without sending it).
- Play racquetball.

2) What are some of the ways that work for you when managing your own healthy venting?

3) It takes me, on average, about 2 hours to "simmer down," restore my connection with myself (balance).

4) About how long does it take you?

Write a number then circle a measure of time: _____ hours/days/months/years

*If you have a difficult time answering this question, measure the amount of time between your argument and your apology (or feelings of regret, or feelings that you

might have gone too far).

**Another way is to measure how long it takes for you to miss the connection you had with the other person before the argument began (you want things back the way they were before the conflict).

Personal Notes and Lessons Learned

CHAPTER THREE
Developing Communication Skills

Communication skills do not resolve conflicts. It is the purpose of good communication skills to create clarity: both rational clarity and emotional clarity. The purpose of communication skills in conflict management is to keep the door of communication open.

The reason good communication skills are so important in conflict management is that you cannot resolve a conflict with someone you are not talking to. Communication skills, then, play an important role in conflict management, but you will need more skills to get you to resolution. In fact, there are three distinct skill sets necessary to be an expert conflict manager: communication skills, resolution skills and negotiation skills. Communication skills are not enough.

One conflict management book I read taught reflective

listening as the skill necessary for resolving conflicts. The author proposed that reflecting back what was said by the angry or disagreeable person, would eventually target what needed to be done to make the situation better and end the conflict. To believe clarity resolves conflict you must assume that lack of clarity is the cause of conflict. However, in the midst of incompatible goals, interests, feelings or principles, clarity that our goals are incompatible does nothing to resolve the incompatibility.

> Keeping communication open is important when managing a healthy venting process.

Reflective listening is an excellent communication skill, but it is not enough to resolve conflicts. "I statements" is another excellent clarity skill, but it will only take you so far when trying to deal with conflict.

Keeping the door of communication open is probably most important when managing a healthy venting process. Often in a conflict you may find yourself having to do both: keep communication open and manage a healthy venting process. I have found my communication skills to be the best way to navigate through a healthy venting process and set me up nicely for using my resolution and negotiation skills.

But be careful. There is big difference between effective venting management and resolving a conflict. Do not think that because venting has been successful the conflict is over. Don't even be seduced into thinking that it is *almost* over. Calm people with great communication skills do not a conflict resolve. Remember, communication skills are only designed to keep the door of communication open. Your resolution skills will get you across that threshold.

Here are five techniques I use to keep the communication door open and move people toward resolution.

- Summarizing and Paraphrasing
- Asking Probing Questions
- Identifying and Naming Emotions
- Validating Whenever Possible
- Finding the Positive Request

The first four are fairly familiar, so I will offer brief descriptions. In my experience, the fifth one is a little known but powerful technique, so I will spend more time with "Finding the Positive Request." If you will master this one, it will change all of your conflict communication for the better.

— Summarizing and Paraphrasing —

Summarizing and paraphrasing are good techniques for keeping the door of communication open. When summarizing, you repeat back the other person's statement using their key words. When paraphrasing you want to pull out some of the toxic language while keeping the substance of the other person's statement or comment.

One of my three girls works at a national coffee chain. One day, frustrated with one of her employees, she shared with me this exchange between the server and a loyal, high volume customer:

> Server: "You could recycle your cups, using the same one when you come back in; or we could rinse out your cup for you when you come in. Every time you come in, you always leave a big mess."

I could summarize this with: "So you would like for me to bring my cups in from my earlier visit to reuse them. You think I leave the place in a mess when I'm here."

There is not much toxic language so let's make the server's language worse:

> Server: "You are a threat to the environment. Everywhere you go a trail of trash follows. Your habits are shortening the life span of the only planet we have. You should be more thoughtful and considerate."

I could paraphrase with: *"So you would like me to recycle."*

Notice that summary and paraphrase do not imply agreement or guilt. By using this technique I keep the other person talking, thereby keeping communication open.

— Asking Probing Questions —

Asking probing questions is a great door-propping technique and critically important when I am managing a healthy venting process. My goal and tone for these questions is to be exploratory. I am trying to find out how this person is seeing the situation, how they are coming to the conclusions they are presenting. In short, I am trying to understand their thinking process.

> You cannot defend yourself and seek to understand the other person at the same time.

WARNING: there is usually someone in the room who wants to understand the other person's thinking process in order to find the flaws in their thinking, do them the favor of pointing this out, and correct this for them. This feeds the conflict and the venting. Don't do this.

To ask in order to correct makes you defensive. You cannot defend yourself and really seek to understand the other person at the same time. Asking in order to correct will often slam the door of communication shut. As soon as you try to correct their understanding, you poorly begin the resolution part of the conflict resolution process. You correct them assuming:

> *"If you had the correct understanding of this situation, then we would not be having this conflict. A correct understanding, which I just happen to have, will resolve this conflict. Listen and I will explain to you where your misunderstanding lies."*

Also please note this is a classic 'the person is the problem' statement.

Correcting their understanding of the situation is not a useful resolution technique. Besides, this is not the resolution stage of the conflict. This is the venting stage. The danger of communication breaking down is very likely. You need to use a technique that will increase the chance of continuing this conversation so you can get to the resolution stage. Keep them talking by asking probing questions.

> **Keep them talking by asking probing questions.**

Think of yourself as an explorer in a strange and wondrous landscape. You are trying to learn your way around this new terrain. You are asking in order to understand them, not in order to fix or correct them.

Some probing questions I might ask the coffee server could be:

> *"Hmmm. You seem very interested in the number of cups I use. Why is that?"*

Or, I could ask,

> *"Why are you so interested in the number of cups I use?"*

For those of you more direct and to the point, this wording will work just fine. I like to soften it just a bit in order to minimize the chance of a defensive response. Some other examples could be:

> *"How is it you think I am using too many cups?"*
> *"What difference does it make how may cups I am using?"*
> *"Doesn't more cups mean more money for your company?"*
> *"It sounds like you take recycling very,*

*very seriously. Why? How did you get so
interested in recycling?"*

Or the smart mouth in me wants to ask:

*"How does the number of cups I use affect
your paycheck?"*
*"How many cups would I be using if I
stopped buying coffee here?"*
*"Would it help you with the mess if I just
didn't come back?"*

I often have to fight my smart-mouth impulse in order to be a great conflict manager. Maybe I should list smart-mouth control as a conflict management technique.

When I ask probing questions, one question leads to another and to another until the other person has a chance to tell me soooo much about themselves. People are often very willing to talk about themselves. After all, I am asking them questions about a subject they are expert on: themselves. I use this to my conflict management advantage.

However, I am continually aware of my tone and my timing. My tone needs to sound like genuine curiosity, inquisitive, exploratory. My timing must not sound interrogative, rapid-fire, badgering.

— Identifying and Naming Emotions —

The ability to identify and name emotions at this stage of the conflict helps me keep doors open and helps me to manage a healthy venting process. Identifying the server's emotions, I could ask:

> *"You seem very upset about something I said or did. Can you tell me what happened?"*
>
> *– or –*
>
> *"I can see you're frustrated. Can you tell me why?"*

Identifying my own emotions can also keep conversation going.

> *"I can see you are upset with me. I feel a little defensive and unappreciated. It would help me if you could explain what I did to upset you."*

IMPORTANT NOTE: Please understand I am in no way suggesting you should stand there and take whatever verbal abuse the other person feels the need to spew out. I am trying to describe a healthy venting process, which suggests you may be in the presence of loud, even antagonistic emotions. These skills can get you through this and into the resolution phase of the conflict. Use your communication skills to keep the door open, manage venting in productive, healthy ways, and set yourself up for the resolution stage of the conflict when you can and for as long as you can.

> If you have to leave to protect yourself and your boundaries, then do so.

I am trying to describe how to manage a healthy venting process. When someone confronts you with verbal abuse (any abuse, really), they are practicing boundary abuse, which is healthy neither for you nor for them. If protecting yourself and your boundaries from abuse means leaving the conversation, then leave and regroup later if you can.

— Emotions and Anger —

Let's talk for a moment about one emotion that is no stranger to conflict communication: anger. Anger begets anger. It is part of the natural process of anger. There is nothing wrong with anger, it is just a feeling; it is not a bad thing. So relax a bit.

Let me explain. Anger is our body's natural warning system of impending danger. When someone angry confronts you, even if they are not yelling, even if they are managing their anger in appropriate ways, your body will respond with anger. An angry person in your office, approaching you, standing in front of you, within your general proximity, is, as far as your body is concerned, impending danger. It is not your body's job to evaluate their threat level, the seriousness or intensity of their anger, to evaluate any likelihood that their anger might produce physical harm; your body's job is simply to warn you. It is your job to process the feeling.

The textbooks describe this as escalating conflict. But, in fact, what is happening is not escalating conflict. It is your body picking up on the other person's anger. Escalation will occur every time two people with poor or negligible conflict skills, unable to process (not suppress) their emotions, engage in a conflict. What the books are describing are two skill-less people in an imbalanced personal state. To describe this as the natural dynamics of conflict is like videotaping a seven year old swinging a baseball bat and describing, in detail, this swinging as an example of how bats are swung.

> Listen to your feelings. Learn what they are trying to tell you.

Listen to your feelings. Your emotions are a valuable source of information in any situation, not the least of which is in a conflict situation. Your body knows things your mind does not know. Listen to your feelings. Learn what they are trying to tell you. Use the information to identify which conflict management techniques and tools to utilize.

There are inappropriate and unhelpful ways to express your anger. In conflict, emotions are only a problem when they overpower and silence the intellect (remember Imbalanced Personal State in Chapter 2?). Anger is only a problem when, instead of listening to and hearing this emotion, we act out and behave inappropriately. Anger itself is not the problem. It's the permission we give ourselves to misbehave when we feel anger that needs to change, not our feelings. The mantra should be "feel the anger and stop the inappropriate behavior," not "stop the anger."

> Anger is only a problem when we behave inappropriately.

Neither anger nor emotions is the problem. So what do we do with emotional outbursts and anger as natural characters in a conflict? Expect them to show up and don't allow them to distract you from your role in managing the conflict. It is the purpose of communication skills to create clear communication: both rationally clear and emotionally clear. If you need further work in this area, find a good therapist to help you.

— Validating Whenever Possible —

In your conflict communication, validate whenever you can. This is another way to keep your communication open. Think back to our coffee server. I could validate the server by saying something like:

> *"I really appreciate your saying something to me about this. Even though you are upset, I am glad you had the courage to speak directly to me about your concern."*

After all, the server could simply talk about me behind my back or spit in my coffee. Or, I could validate her perspective with something like:

> *"Wow, the way you describe it, I would be upset too."*

Note that in stating it this way, I am not agreeing with the server's assessment of the situation. I can validate without necessarily agreeing.

I was in a committee meeting once, where during the conversation one of the committee members got so mad at me, he

> Validate a healthy venting process and a healthy response to anger.

got up from the table and left the room. You could feel the tension in the room. The rest of us continued the conversation. A few minutes later he returned to the meeting and to the conversation. At the end of the meeting, I turned to him and thanked him for caring enough about our relationship to leave the room rather than "attack" me.

I validated his healthy venting process, his healthy response to his anger. We still work together on some things and we still do not always see eye-to-eye on issues.

Consider:

> *"You are right on that point."*
> *"I agree with you there."*
> *"I couldn't agree more."*
> *"We agree on the issues, but we see them quite differently."*
> *"I can see how you might see that working."*

Remember, this is not a technique designed to set them up or to offer a back-handed compliment. Validate whenever you can, emphasis on 'whenever.'

In some conflict management circles, we refer to this as the "thank you" technique:

> *"I want to thank you for coming to me."*
> *"I want to thank you for your honesty."*
> *"I want to thank you for the respectful way you are handling this situation."*
> *"I want to thank you for not being passive-aggressive."*
> *"I want to thank you for valuing our relationship."*

Validation can be a moment of shock and surprise to the angry or emotional person. They are expecting a fight. In fact, they came in prepared for one. They practiced all last night, reviewing in their head powerful come-backs. (Don't tell me you never did this.) Agreement or validation on a point is not what they expect. It throws their "script" off; they have to regroup and often to rethink a response to my unexpected validation. It is in this momentary opening where communication has a chance to grow into conversation, moving from debate to discussion and on to dialogue.

— Finding the Positive Request —

This last technique is harder to learn. Once you learn it, it is easy to use. Of the five techniques I am going over here, this one is probably the one I use the most. It does several powerful things, not all of which I will be able to go into here. Right now, let's see if my skills are up to the challenge of explaining this difficult technique with sufficient clarity.

> Inside every criticism is a positive request.

Inside every single criticism is a positive request. I don't care what the criticism is, a positive request lies within it. The beauty is, most criticism comes within the context of conflict. Your job, then, as a manager of conflict, is to find the positive request.

The positive request is not, I repeat, not, putting a positive spin on the criticism. The other day, a colleague and I were at lunch when the cashier made a comment criticizing the gas shortage in our area. My colleague did not miss a beat. "Yes, but the traffic is so much better now." This is an example of putting a positive spin on a criticism. This is NOT the technique I am trying to teach you here.

The positive request technique is a translation skill, not a point of view skill. You will need to learn to translate "criticism language" into "positive request language." Let's start with a simple example.

In most training seminars, someone in the room will say: "Man, is it cold in here!" This is a criticism of the room temperature. We all know the positive request translation. "Would you please turn the heat up?"

This is a translation skill. Like any translation, accuracy may require the use of more words than the number of words used in the original language. Your goal is to translate the criticism into "positive request language," using as many words as necessary to capture the request within the "criticism language." Like any mastery of another language, perfecting this skill takes practice.

This technique works with any criticism.

"You are the worst manager we have ever had."

"You never listen."
"You are a miserable and worthless human being."
"This project is a complete waste of time."
"Life sucks."

Your job is to find the positive request.

"So, you would like to have a better manager."
"You would like to be with someone who listens more."
"So, you would enjoy being around happy human beings."
"You like to work on important projects."
"You wish life was better."

Three things I want you note about this technique: 1) if you get it wrong, communication continues. 2) When done well, the focus of the conversation shifts to where it needs to be. And 3) the temptation to slide immediately into resolution is dangerously strong.

1) Getting it Wrong

Remember, the goal is to keep the door of communication open. If my translation attempt is a dismal failure and the other person corrects me, then communication continues.

> *Criticism: "This project is a complete waste*
> *of time."*
> *First translation attempt: "You like to work*
> *on important projects."*
> *Correction: "No. It is not that it has to be an*
> *important project. It's just that I don't think*
> *this project is going to do what management*
> *believes it will do."*

Notice that communication continued. The door is open for me to follow up by asking a probing question. Say, something like:

> *"So, what do you think would work better?"*

Though my translation is wrong, I still accomplish my goal. The person in conflict with me usually will not hesitate to correct me. The door is still open.

2) Doing it Well

When done well, the focus of the conversation shifts to the only two things the criticizing person can control.

Criticism: "You never listen."
Translation attempt: "So, you would like to
be with someone who listens more."
Critic's response: "Yes. That is what I want."

Notice that the criticism, "You never listen" focuses on me. I am the recipient of the criticism, the subject of the sentence. The person in conflict with me is pointing an imaginary finger in my face. The shift comes in the translation. "So, you would like to be with someone who listens more." Here it comes, "Yes. That is what I want." Who are they talking about now? In the third line, the critic is the subject of the sentence. The critic is now talking about themselves instead of me. Themselves; the only thing they have control over.

— The Number One Mistake Novices Make —

Summarizing instead of translating is the number one mistake novices make when practicing this technique.

Criticism: "You never listen."
Translation attempt: "So, you don't think I
listen well."
Critic's response: "I know you don't listen
well."

My translation attempt is a summary, not a translation. The first line, the criticism, points an imaginary finger in my face. The second line, because it is a summary of the criticism, also focuses on me. "So, you don't think I listen." Therefore the third line becomes further criticism of me. Notice that the shift to the critic does not take place when I summarize.

Let's do them all:

> *Criticism: "You are the worst manager we*
> *have ever had."*
> *"So you don't think I am a good manager" is*
> *a summary.*
> *"So, you would like to have a better*
> *manager" is a translation.*

> *Criticism: "You never listen."*
> *"So, you don't think I listen well" is a*
> *summary.*
> *"You would like to be with someone who*
> *listens more" is a translation.*

> *Criticism: "You are a miserable and*
> *worthless human being."*
> *"You think I am a miserable, worthless*
> *human being" is a summary.*
> *"So, you would enjoy being around happy*

human beings" is a translation.

Criticism: "This project is a complete waste of time."
"You hate this project" is a summary.
"You like to work on important projects" is a translation.

Criticism: "Life sucks."
"You hate your life" is a summary.
"You wish life was better" is a translation.

If you compare the differences, one thing you will note is the absence of the "I" in the translation. Another thing you might notice in the last two examples is that while the summary sounds a lot like the translation, the summary is still negative. Remember, you are looking to uncover the positive request. Practice this technique and work on staying away from summarizing.

3) Temptation

The third thing I want you to be aware of is the natural, powerful temptation to slide immediately into problem solving and solution suggesting.

Criticism: "You never listen."

Translation: "You would like to be with someone who listens more."

Response: "Yes, I would."

Temptation: "Ok. I'll listen. What do you want to say?"

> **Do not slide immediately into problem solving and solution suggesting. Resist the urge!**

I cannot warn you enough of the overwhelming power of this temptation in our culture. By my experience, we all seem to be excellent problem solvers and solution suggesters, but this is not what resolving this conflict requires right now. Be very careful not to give in to this temptation by suggesting a solution at this point. Unfortunately, this is a mistake almost everybody ends up making.

Using the temptation phrase will keep the door of communication open, and in that regard it is an excellent comment. However, if you believe you have resolved this conflict by offering to listen, then you will be mistaken and in for an uncomfortable surprise. What is causing this conflict is not the fact that you do not listen, but the fact that the person confronting you does not feel heard; two very different things. So, will listening to them make them feel heard? Maybe, but probably not. Why are they not feeling heard? What would have to happen for this person to feel heard? What were the circumstances in the past when they felt heard? These are need-exploration questions.

At the end of the communication stage and the beginning of the resolution stage of this conflict is need exploration. Do not use Finding the Positive Request as your segue into solving the problem. Use it to launch need exploration. The most important and least-known resolution skill is need exploration. Let's look at how it is done and what it means to managing conflicts.

— **Communication Skills Worksheet** —

Positive request exercise:

1) List as many criticisms as you can think of below:

2) Translate the criticisms list above into positive requests:

3) Identify the translation attempts below with either an 'S' for summary, or with a 'T' for translation:

Criticism: "You are a moron."

a. _____ Translation attempt: "So, you think you are

smarter than me."

Criticism: "I can't stand whiny people."

b. _____ Translation attempt: "You want to be around upbeat people."

Criticism: "This book is stupid."

c. _____ Translation attempt: "You don't think this book is worth reading."

Criticism: "Tomorrow is going to be a bad day."

d. _____ Translation attempt: "You would rather tomorrow not come."

Criticism: "All politicians lie."

e. _____ Translation attempt: "You believe politicians cannot tell the truth."

Criticism: "I don't like you."

f. _____ Translation attempt: "You wish I was dead."

4) Go to my website at www.answerkeys.drrickv.com to get a free copy of the answer key.

5) Take the summaries in exercise number three and

turn them into translations:

a. Translation:

b. Translation:

c. Translation:

d. Translation:

e. Translation:

f. Translation:

6) Go to my website at www.answerkeys.drrickv.com to get a free copy of the answer key.

Personal Notes and Lessons Learned

CHAPTER FOUR
Exploring Needs

We are great problem solvers. We are lousy need explorers. I will demonstrate this with a true story I adapted from Fisher and Ury's book *Getting to Yes*[1] about two kids arguing over an orange.

You have two kids, one orange: conflict. What do you do? In every training seminar the group always solves this problem in a second or less. "Cut the orange in half." Problem solved. Conflict ended. Get back to whatever important thing you were doing.

The danger here, the danger every time you problem solve, is you solve a problem that does not exist. I see it happen so often that I have taken to distinguishing between a solution and a resolution when I teach.

1   Fisher, R.,Ury, W., & Patton, B. (1991). "*Getting to Yes: Negotiating agreement without giving in*" (2nd ed.) New York: Penguin

Two things happen when you solve problems that do not exist. First, the conflict does not go away. It goes underground to surface later. And second, the people you have "helped" end up resenting you, the problem solver, for both your resolution process and its outcome.

The kids are arguing over an orange. By focusing on the orange, it appears we can only solve this problem by splitting the orange so they both get part of it. However, the problem was not having only one orange. The problem is with the kids. Let me explain by looking at their behavior when you give them each their half of the orange.

> **Do not solve a nonexistent problem. Instead, find the underlying need.**

The one child took the orange, peeled it and ate the inside of the orange. The other child took the orange, peeled it, threw the inside away and used the peel for a science project.

What every problem solver in my seminars assumes is that the kids want to eat the orange. And every problem solver in that room ends up solving a problem that does not exist. Instead of solving their problem, let's explore their needs.

What is the need of the kid who ate the inside of the orange? The need is not the orange, it is hunger. How many different ways are there to meet this child's hunger need without the orange? There are many, many options available to meet this child's hunger need.

> *"Honey, I just baked a chocolate cake. It's in the kitchen; help yourself."*
>
> — *or* —
>
> *"Honey, you can have anything you can find in the refrigerator."*

But what if the child's need is nutritional? We still have many ways available to us to meet that need. The chocolate cake is not one of them. This leads us to a third secret about managing conflict.

Conflict Management Secret #3: There is ALWAYS more than one way to meet a need.

This is why resolution skills resolve conflicts. You exponentially increase the chance of finding a resolution by creating multiple options that will meet the person's need.

What is the need of the child who threw away the inside of the orange? The need could be succeeding in the science project; it could be getting the teacher's attention; it could be not failing the class; it could

> **Resolve conflict by meeting the person's need.**

be getting into a well known science program or scholarship; it could be impressing a girl in class or on the project. Whatever the need, and only the child will be able to tell you, there are ways to meet any of the above needs that do not necessarily employ the single orange they are fighting over.

Everybody comes to the conflict with an "orange." It is their single solution (remember Single Solution Mindset in Chapter 2?) they bring to the table. They focus on the orange, they demand the orange, and life will not be worth living unless they get the orange. They have named one possible option for resolving this conflict, elevated it to the best solution in their mind, and made it their demand when in fact their "orange" is simply one option.

The "orange" does something for them. It fixes something in their life. It makes something better. Your job, as a need explorer is to figure that out. The only clue you have to what their need really is, is the demand they are making, is their "orange." So let's explore their "orange" to see what future it provides them.

> The "orange" does something for them. It fixes something in their life.

Now that you know the future behavior of the arguing kids (this is a hint pointing to resolution skills we will get into when we learn about conflict's timeline in Chapter 5), lets rewind the tape and go back to the beginning.

Two kids, one orange; what do you do?

Ask a question. The number one characteristic of a good need explorer is to ask a ton of questions. I will give you three questions that will help you in your practice as a need explorer. But first let me point out the one question that never works for me.

That one question is: "What do you need?"

Does it not make sense that, if knowing their need gets me closer to a resolution, then asking them what they need is the perfect question? In my experience, it never works. The reason it never works is that they do not know what their need is. The reason they do not know their own need is...here it is....they are lousy need explorers.

Let's ask the kids what they need.

Parent: "Sweetheart, what do you need?"

Here is the answer I get, every time, from every "kid" I meet stuck in a conflict:

Kid: "The Orange."

One major reason people get stuck in conflict is they do not know what need they are fighting to meet. The number one reason communication skills do not resolve conflict is they will not get you to their needs. Need exploration is a resolution skill. It is hard to do. It will take a great deal of practice (and failure) on your part to learn it, and you will be on your own practicing it. This skill is not modeled anywhere for you. It is not modeled at work, at school. You will not see it modeled for you on TV, by actors, by athletes, on commercials, in a sitcom, etc.

Some people find it helpful to distinguish between what the arguing kids "want" and their "need." If this is helpful to you, start here.

> *Parent: "No honey, the orange is what you want. You would like very much to have that orange, but you do not need that orange. A need is something that satisfies a basic human hunger deep inside all of us. Meeting your need will help you thrive as a human being. So, rather than tell me what you want, tell me what you need."*
>
> *Kid: "Uh?!"*

The distinction between "want" and "need" works better if you keep it in your head, using it to guide your exploration skills. While in many ways it is a useless practical distinction, because it tends to minimize their stated expectations and outcomes, it can help the explorer practice their skill.

I was working with a couple to modify their divorce decree. In my private meeting with the wife, I asked her, "If you could have anything you wanted here today, what would you ask for?"

> *Former wife: "I would want this first divorce decree torn to shreds!"*
>
> *Me: "How would that help you here today?"*
>
> *Former wife: "Every time he got on his high horse, I would have a way to stop him!"*
>
> *Me: "Ok. But how would having a way to stop him help you?"*
>
> *Former wife: "He wouldn't be able to pick at me about every little thing. I wouldn't need to hire an attorney all the time, draining my bank account."*
>
> *Me: "So, let's say you had a document that gave you all of the power to stop him. How would THAT help you? What would that power give you?"*
>
> *Former wife: "It would give me peace of mind."*
>
> *Me: "So if we could find a way here today to get you peace of mind, a lasting, consistent*

peace of mind, you would be happy. You
would sign a resolution that provides you
with peace of mind?"
Former wife: "Yes."

Notice how hard it was for her to talk about her need. She does not know how to get there. I have to ask enough questions, in many different ways, in order to discover her need. I still have to ask her what "peace of mind" looks like, and I know a different divorce decree is one option that could begin to do that, but now I know her need. This is a hard skill to learn, made harder by the fact that the people you are exploring with cannot effectively help you.

> Ask many questions in different ways to discover the need.

One time I did need exploration with a divorcing wife. Her attorney was adamant about applying aggressive tactics in order to bend her husband's will to agree with to their demands.

Attorney: "We are going to crush him in
court. We are going to drag out evidence of
his various affairs, his anger and abuse, his
irresponsibility with their family finances."
Me, to the wife: "What do you want here

today?"

Wife: "I want custody of the kids and for him to keep the mortgage on the second house he bought for his business!"

Attorney: "And if he doesn't agree with our demands, then he will have to pay even more money as we drag this out in court."

Me, to wife: "If you could have anything... If you knew that whatever you asked for this morning, it would be granted to you, no questions asked, what would you ask for?"

Wife: "I just want this man out of my life."

Me, to wife: "So if we could get this man out of your life today, would you be happy with a resolution that did that for you?"

Wife: "Yes."

Me, to wife and attorney: "So if this gets dragged out through court, would it mean this man would still be in your life during all this time?"

Wife: "Yes."

Her need was to be set free from this man. By getting her need on the table it could now inform every decision she made. It also gave her focus to make decisions that helped her. She was able to distinguish between those decisions that helped her and the tactics being used by her attorney.

By focusing on her need, I was able to defuse the value of the attorney's aggressive tactics and empower her to make decisions in her own best interest.

Notice the number of questions I asked. Notice the future direction many of those questions took. To resolve this conflict, I needed to know the future, so I had to create questions that painted as vivid a picture of the future as possible.

— Three Questions to Get You Started —

Here are some questions I use in need exploration. First, I ask them to tell me what they want. This will get their demand on the table. They will state their single solution here; they will present their "orange." In the examples above I would ask this question as, "If you could have anything you want, the best of all possible worlds, what would you ask for?"

> The first question is designed to get their demand out in the open.

So the first question is designed to get their demand out in the open. I have learned that what they say, more often than not, will not be their need. So don't be fooled. It may be their best of all possible worlds but, in this situation, it is still simply their "orange". Remember, people do not know how to do need exploration on themselves.

Once I have their "orange" on the table, I must explore some characteristics of this "orange" to try to determine what it will do for them. So the second question I will often ask is, "Why do you want 'the orange?'"

There are two types of "why" questions: One "why" question wants to know the reasons behind something; the other "why" question wants to know the purpose for something. The need explorer is asking, "For what purpose are you demanding this orange?" Inevitably, your person in conflict will answer by giving you the reasons they deserve the "orange."

In the divorce examples above, I tried to get to this by asking, "How will this help you?" Notice how bad the former wife was at need exploration. She kept telling me how it would affect his behavior, not how it would help her. The more someone focuses on the other person (remember the person is the problem?), the further away they are getting

> Stay focused! Don't be distracted by the answers you are given.

from knowing their own need. A need explorer's job is to stay focused; do not get distracted by the answers they give you. Had I explored any of the answers she gave me, they would have taken me far afield from what I was looking for. Therefore, one of the skills a need explorer must develop is knowing what not to listen to. The danger with listening skills alone is the tangential tracks taken by listening to bad answers given by people who do not know how to explore their own need.

I can take the "for what purpose" question deeper by asking an impact question. "What impact will it have if you do not get this "orange"? One child tells me, "I will starve to death!" The other child tells me, "I will fail my science project." Both answers paint a picture of a future event. I am closer to their needs.

I can ask this same question, but from the opposite point of view. Instead of asking, "What impact will it have if you DO NOT get this "orange?" I will ask, "What impact will it have if you DO get this "orange?" Often, in asking both questions I get a nuance in their answer that will get me even closer to discovering their need.

Once I think I have someone's need, I can play around with it, trying to get a clearer picture of their future. With the need will come multiple options. Sifting through several options will also create clarity for both the need explorer and the other person.

It is not unusual for someone to experience surprise in the moment of need discovery. Often at the end of a need exploration exercise the person I am working with will have a kind of epiphany. It is as though a light

> Discover
> the need
> and several
> options become
> apparent.

goes on. Knowing their need empowers them. It takes their focus off the other person as the problem and gets them focused on the only thing they can control: their own attitude and their own actions.

I was working with another divorcing couple who were entrenched in their pain and stuck in their single solution mindset. They had been in this position for a long time, seeing no way out of the situation. Their prolonged fighting had begun to spill over onto their friends and family, creating a widening circle of pain for everyone pulled into their divorce. It was then that I was called in.

Exploring needs, I discovered one person was leaving the relationship in order to stay healthy. The relationship was hurting their mental and emotional health and they were leaving the relationship in order to regain their health. If health was the need, and not moving on would hurt their health, then the question was, "How important are your demands if they cost you your health?" "Are the demands that are keeping you two stuck together, trapped in this unending cycle of disagreement, worth the continued harm to your health?" "If you could end this today, would your journey to health begin?"

Discovering need empowers decision making. A couple of sessions later, the husband came to our session with clarity. "I want to begin my journey of health." He wanted health (his need) more than he wanted his "orange" (his single solution).

One last example: I was doing divorce coaching. The wife was my client and we were doing need exploration in my office. She and her husband were stuck on who would get the house. She spent the first 20 minutes explaining to me why she should get the house (her "orange"). She answered my first few questions with the psychological and emotional benefits getting the house would have for the kids. Her focus on the kids indicated to me I did not yet have her need.

I knew this was not her need because the focus was on the kids and not on her. "How would the house help you (not the kids)?" When our need exploration was complete she was surprised to realize it was not the physical house she needed. She had spent all this time arguing for the physical four walls they called the house. That was not it at all. She needed several things, and once she realized what they were she was ready to negotiate for her needs. She could give up the physical four walls if certain conditions were met. Those conditions could vary.

There were multiple ways to meet those conditions. What she discovered was that the physical house was only one of the ways to meet those conditions. Meet the conditions and you meet the needs. The house could go.

> When a person discovers their own need, it changes the way they negotiate.

Her discovery of her needs changed the way she negotiated. It changed the way she fought. Discovering needs will change the dynamics of the conflict. Need exploration skills took me across the threshold of the door my communication skills kept open. By discovering her needs, I now stood squarely in the room of resolution.

— Summary —

In Chapter 2 I introduced you to three dynamics associated with conflict communication: the person becomes the problem, a single solution mindset, and an imbalanced personal state. In the last chapter we looked at five communication techniques for facilitating a healthy venting process and getting one back into a balanced personal state.

Need exploration will get you around the other two conflict communication dynamics. Exploring a person's need, you take their focus off of the other person as the problem and get them talking about themselves. Discovering a person's need will take them out of a single solution mindset. There are many options available for meeting a need, not just the one they have made into their demand, not just the "orange."

Three questions will get you started as a need explorer:

1) What do you what?

2) Why do you want this?

3) What impact will it have on your life if you get this

(or don't get this)?

Remember, we all have basic human needs, as Maslow states in his hierarchy of needs. Many of the needs that drive us into a conflict reflect some kind of threat to our basic human needs. Listen for these things when you explore. Try to drive the questioning deeper and deeper. Don't just settle for the first answer they present to you. It is more than likely that they will not be able to tell you what their needs are because they don't know how to apply this skill to themselves.

Practice on yourself. After all, you are human; you have basic needs. Practice looking deep within yourself and asking what it is you want. Why do you want this? How will it help you? What will it do for you? And follow up with: What will be the impact on your life if you do not get what you are asking for or demanding? As you get better at applying this skill to yourself, your skill as a resolver of conflict will improve.

— Need Exploration Worksheet —

I. One Option Exercise

1) Make a list of as many different demands as you can think of, or ask someone to role play with you for a moment and make a demand of you. For example:

a.   I want 10,000.00 dollars!
b.   I want you to leave!
c.   I expect you to be on time!
d.   I need you to take me seriously!
e.
f.
g.
h.
i.
j.
k.
l.

2) Read the demands listed above out loud. For every demand listed above, say to yourself, "That's one option." I want you to train yourself to hear demands as "one option." The more you practice this, the easier it will be for you to start your need exploration process.

II. Exploring Need

1) There is a country song by Trent Tomlinson titled *Drunker Than Me*. Go to my website at www.answerkeys. drrickv.com to read a copy of the lyrics.

2) Let's look at this song, listen to this man's problem and practice our Need Exploration skills on him.

    a.   His girlfriend (or wife) seems to be getting drunker and drunker the more they go out. At first she kept it to a little drunk, but now she is getting really drunk.

    b.   His problem isn't her getting drunker. It is her getting drunker than he.

    c.   His single solution is for her to stop getting drunker than he. (Also, please note he has made her the problem throughout the song.)

What does he want? What is his demand? What is his "orange?"

For her to stop getting drunker than he.

Why does he want this? To what end is he asking for this?

He wants one of them to be sober enough to "get the keys, get the phone, get the bill, and call a cab." He does not want to be the "responsible" one because it will kill his buzz.

What impact will it have on him if there is no one sober enough to get the keys, get the phone, get the bill, and call a cab?

There will not be anyone responsible for getting the keys to the car, getting their phone, getting the bill, and calling a cab. Their keys will not be gotten, the phone will not be gotten, the bill will not be gotten, and no one will call a cab.

What impact will it have on him if he DOES have someone sober enough to get the keys, get the phone, get the bill, and call a cab?

There will be someone responsible for getting the keys to the car, getting their phone, getting the bill, and calling a cab.

What could happen if there is no one responsible or sober enough to do these things? He states he does not want to be the responsible one because it will kill his buzz. His single solution is for her to sacrifice her good time in order for him to have a good time. Her not getting drunker than he fixes something for him. Both of them having a good time could jeopardize something. Can you now guess what his need might be?

His need is: SAFETY

3) How many ways can you think of that would keep both drunks safe? Make a list of ten options for keeping these two people safe when getting drunk:

a. She not get drunker than he.

b.

c.

d.

e.

f.

g.

h.

i.

j.

Notice: One option is for her to not get drunker than he. Remember, his demand is one option. It is one option only. By making it his "orange," he is setting up an ultimatum for her that, in all likelihood, will damage their relationship. Now he has a list of multiple options available to him that will get him what he needs and, at the same time, possibly put less strain on their relationship. He gets to choose which option will work best for him.

4) To get a free list of the options I generated for this exercise, go to my website www.answerkeys.drrickv.com.

Personal Notes and Lessons Learned

CHAPTER FIVE

The Time to Fight

Conflict follows a timeline. There is a past, a present, and a future. Only two of these can be negotiated. Do you know which two? In almost every seminar I do, everyone gets this question wrong. People tend to assume: present and future, because the past can't be changed. But this answer is wrong.

Everyone in conflict negotiates the past. "You didn't do what you said you would." "You did something you were not supposed to do." Or in a board meeting I was in, I heard two people negotiating the past with, "All I said was...." "Well it sounded to me like you were...." Listen when people are fighting. Better yet, listen when you are fighting. Count the number of past tense verbs in your statements.

The assumption is that if I can get you to agree with me about what "really" happened, our argument will be over.

— Negotiating the Past —

I set up a typical conflict scenario in my seminars: "You didn't take out the garbage again like you said you would." From here I can get into the skills necessary for getting to resolution of this argument. One of my male students took issue with my quick movement away from the past. "Wait a minute. My wife thinks I screwed up and is upset with me. If I can explain what happened, then she would understand and not be upset with me any more." He wanted to create a narrative that set his actions in a context that would not be "upset worthy." She would forgive him and all would be well with the world once again.

Keep in mind, his narrative was not a lie. He was not trying to make something up to get out of trouble. No, his narrative of the past is true. It is true from his perspective. His wife has another perspective on the past event. It is important to realize we, as effective conflict managers, are not looking for truth. In fact, my experience has taught me that the truth does not resolve conflicts. Convincing her of his point of view, of the "truth," would not necessarily change her frustration. By focusing on the "truth" of the situation, he misses the need his wife was trying to express.

> There is a past, a present, and a future. Only two of these can be negotiated.

Negotiating the past always leads to defensiveness. By negotiating the past he feels he must defend his actions, and she feels she must defend her interpretation of his actions. The resolution of this conflict does not lie in the past "facts." It lies in the future, which introduces the fourth secret for managing conflict.

Conflict Management Secret #4: All resolution is future oriented.

Therefore, in any conflict you want to negotiate the future if you wish for a resolution. Only two time elements can be negotiated in any conflict: the past and the future. Negotiating the past always leads to defensiveness, so negotiate the future. That's where the resolution lies.

— Getting Out of the Past and into the Future —

This is the skill most people don't have. I will offer three questions for navigating through a conflict keeping the future in mind. However, I must warn you now. There is nothing magical about either the questions, or the order in which you ask them. For teaching purposes, the introduction of these questions will sound very mechanical and static. They are not; and if you try to apply this in a mechanical, static, linear structure, you will more than likely escalate the conflict and probably close the door of communication.

These questions are woven into a larger dialogue by a skilled conflict resolver who is paying close attention to the nature and dynamics of the conflict. Knowing the questions is not the skill. I can teach you the questions in a few short pages. The skill comes in knowing how conflict works and weaving them into the conflict appropriately enough to achieve the goal of resolution.

Looking at the "you didn't take out the garbage again" scenario, the first question you want to ask to get to the future is about the past, "What happened?"

The exact words are not important here. What you want to know is what happened to cause her to feel the way she does. Something about your not taking out the garbage caused her to be upset. What was it?

Are you confused? I said negotiating the past would lead to defensiveness, not resolution. So why am I telling you to explore the past? Two reasons: 1) the hurt person needs to talk about what happened to them. And 2) you are looking for a baseline for their emotional response.

> Explore the past, but do not attempt to negotiate it.

I am asking you to not negotiate the past. Some read from this that the past is irrelevant, useless to the resolution process and should be ignored. This is a mistake and discounts the emotional dynamics of conflict. I am asking you to explore the past, not negotiate it. You can explore it without having to defend your version of it. If you begin to defend, to correct, to offer an alternative narrative, then you have slipped into negotiating the past.

Exploring the past means you are asking questions about how she understands the circumstance. Understanding her perspective on the situation gives you the baseline you need to move forward. If you are going the change the relational damage between the two of you, then you need to understand how she came to feel the way she does. The resolution is directly related to changing how she feels.

This is why seeking to eliminate emotions is a disastrous suggestion; why, by ignoring emotions in conflict, we tend to do conflict so poorly. If a proposed solution does not affect her negative feelings, then it is not a good resolution to this conflict. That means that one of the tests of a good resolution to any conflict is its impact on the way someone is feeling toward you and/or the situation. But we are getting ahead to the third question when we haven't even introduced the second and most important question.

— The 2nd Question: The Most Important of All —

The second question is the pivot point between the past and the future. This is the question you have in the back of your mind from the very first moment the conflict begins. "What are you asking me to do?"

"What are you asking me to do?" is a future-oriented question. As soon as the other person answers this question you are negotiating the future. But let me tell you what will not work.

Being the confident conflict manager that I am, I would try to shorten the conflict dynamic by asking the future question first. Here is what happened when I did not pay attention to how conflict works. When I went for the pivot first, wanting to get over the past and get to the juice, the other person could not answer the question. After, blundering through this several times, I began to notice a pattern. It was as though they needed to get the past off their chest before they could accept any invitation into the future.

What I concluded from this is that people who are hurt, frustrated by my actions, want me to understand first that I have caused them pain. They want me to know, to understand, and in most cases, to admit, that I did something wrong and what I did hurt them.

> People who have been hurt want their pain to be acknowledged.

I no longer "cut to the chase" when resolving conflict. But you are welcome to try. If your experience is anything like mine, then what you will find is, even if you ask the second question first, they will answer the first question. Let me illustrate:

> *"You did not take out the garbage out last night, like you promised. You always forget, and you always promise to remember it the next time. You are not dependable."*

> *"What is it you are asking me to do?"*

> *"I shouldn't have to ask you to do anything. You should take responsibility for the things you say you are going to do. I can't even trust your word when you promise to do something. Obviously, just because you promise something does not mean you will keep your word. You forgot to take out the garbage again! Even your promise is worthless."*

Notice she did not answer the future question. This means she is still in phase one of the conflict timeline: the past. You, as a good conflict manager, must join her there if you hope to move forward. It is here, where your communication skills (Chapter 3) should be applied to keep the door of communication open. It is in this phase of the conflict where communication skills are the most valuable.

Do not force the future. She needs to vent, she needs to get this off her chest. The conflict cannot move to the future or to the resolution phase until she is able to do this. This is what I was referring to above when I said it is important to explore the past without negotiating it because she needs to talk about what you "did" to her.

Stay in the past as an explorer for as long as necessary. Periodically test the waters with a future-oriented question. Eventually, she will answer question two for you and negotiating the future begins.

> *"You did not take out the garbage last night, like you promised. You always forget, and you always promise to remember it the next time. You are not dependable."*

> *"What is it you are asking me to do?"*

> *"I want you to do the dishes! I had to take out the garbage, what you were supposed to do, so now I want you do the dishes!"*

— Negotiating the Future —

Notice we have a proposal for a future action. This action is offered as a recompense for the failed past action. We are now going to negotiate what the future will look like. Will it look like me washing the dishes? Or will it look like me not washing the dishes, watching the game instead?

If you say "OK" here and agree to wash the dishes, you

will fail as a good conflict manager and will be making a huge mistake. This mistake is born mainly out of conflict avoidance.

Most people will make the mistake of going for the "OK" here. "If doing the dishes is what it will take to repair the relationship, then I will do it." But this is not what it will take to repair the relationship. What is required here is not an "OK," but a conflict manager who can do need exploration. It is phase two of the conflict where your need exploration skills (Chapter 4) best apply.

How do you know whether or not her request for washing the dishes is simply a punishment? If it is a punishment for not taking out the garbage, then two things will happen if you agree: 1) you will be agreeing to being punished, and 2) her feelings about the situation will not be affected.

You should never agree to punishment. You should agree to meet her need. Agreeing to her punishment will not change the emotional baseline. In fact, it will reinforce the emotional baseline. Obviously, her assessment and her feelings of distrust must be right, if you agree to the punishment.

Doing the dishes is her "orange." What will the orange fix for her? You must explore what she wants, why she wants it, and what impact it will have on her life if she does not get the dishes washed.

One of the impacts you need to consider in your need exploration is whether or not it will change the way she is feeling about you and the situation. One of the tests as to whether or not her proposal is, in fact, a punishment or a need is its impact on her feelings. If it is a punishment, then her feeling of satisfaction will be short lived; she will not really feel as though this issue has been resolved. And accepting a punishment as a resolution gives her permission to continue punishing you over this issue.

> Never agree to punishment. Instead, agree to meet the need.

You must get to the need if you hope to resolve this. In the many cases where I have spontaneously played out this scenario, the typical course of this conflict goes to feeling overworked and underappreciated. The demand to do the dishes is an effort to enforce a reduction or redistribution of the workload (a workload that was unfairly distributed by your forgetting to take out the garbage again, leaving it for her to do, again!).

If the problem is an overdemanding workload, then the need is to find a way to lessen the workload. Remember, there is always more than one way to meet a need (Conflict Management Secret #3). How many different resolution possibilities can you think of that would lessen, lighten, or even completely remove her workload? In my experience, people can think of many.

Imagine after need exploration and negotiating what

the future might look like if you offer to do all of the house-work for the evening. Suppose you propose she goes out tonight with her girlfriends and you take care of the kids and laundry tonight. Do you suppose, if you have indeed applied your need exploration skills effectively, she would reject such a proposal?

What if your proposal went so far as to even negotiate that you would do everything tonight, but not do the dish-es? Do you think she would accept such an offer?

Most people sense danger here and say, "No," she would not accept the no dishes offer. In fact, fear suggests that she would counter propose: the kids, the laundry, the dishes, her freedom tonight, and for the rest of the week. And we are back to punishment.

— The Third Question: Benefit —

This happens because most people fail to ask the third question: the benefit question. "How will doing this benefit you, as well as benefit me?"

The benefit question safeguards against punishment.

> *"How will my doing all of the chores and*
> *your going out with your girlfriends for a*
> *week benefit you?"*

> *"It's the least you should do for putting me in*

this position again."

"I understand, I upset you and I am sorry for that, but how would my doing these things benefit you?"

"I would get a week off from the chores and get some free time."

"How would getting a week off from the chores and some free time benefit you? And how would doing these things benefit me?"

There are five components of a commitment: it is well planned, operational, bilateral, realistic and having positive and negative consequences.[1] If you are going to make a commitment to a future action plan, then consider at least the bilateral nature of commitment. If I do what you are asking, then what are you willing to do in exchange for my doing what you ask? What benefit is there for me in doing what you are asking me to do?

I am not saying I am unwilling to do what you are asking. I just want to insure that doing what you ask will accomplish my desired outcome. In other words, why would I

1   Fisher, R.,Ury, W., & Patton, B. (1991). *"Getting to Yes: Negotiating agreement without giving in"* (2nd ed.) New York: Penguin

do all of the chores for a week, giving you a night out every night next week only for you to remain angry with me about the garbage? This is one of the reasons finding the baseline was so important. The baseline tells me what happened and why she is upset. This is what I am willing to put effort into changing. I want my future action to affect her feelings in a positive way. Doing them with no assurance of affective change is a mistake and promotes punishment.

> *"How will my doing all of the chores and you going out with your girlfriends for a week benefit you?"*

> *"It's the least you should do for putting me in this position again."*

> *"I understand, I upset you and I am sorry for that, but how would my doing these things benefit you?"*

> *"I would get a week off from the chores and get some free time."*

> *"How would doing these things benefit me?"*

> *"You would see what it is like to have to do all the work around here and appreciate how*

hard it is."

"OK. I am willing to consider doing what you are asking me to do, but if I do will you, then, no longer be mad with me about the garbage?"

Usually, the benefit question goes something like this: "I will be willing to see that the chores are done and you can take the rest of the night off to relax. I am sorry for the problems my irresponsibility has caused you, and I don't want you to stay mad at me. If you get the night off, would you forgive me for the garbage?"

The point was not the garbage. The garbage was a symptom of a larger problem. The problem was her feeling stuck with all the work around the house and your being oblivious to what it takes to keep up with it all. She wants you to get it. She wants you to understand and appreciate all that she does. She wants you to get off your lazy hiney and pitch in. It's not about the garbage; it's not about the dishes; it's about your getting it. And a night off would help her and maybe indicate you understand a little what she has to do every night. If you can't get there, you will not resolve this conflict.

> The garbage is not the point. It is just a symptom of the problem.

Most people completely fail doing the benefit phase. They agree to do the dishes, thinking they are making a (bilateral) commitment, only to find out that doing what she asked did nothing to change her mood, feelings, or attitude toward you. The result is twofold: You resent having agreed to doing it. "Why do I even try? I did what you asked, and I still have to sleep on the couch?" And she stays unsatisfied and angry because she got what she asked for instead of what she needed.

The next time you two argue, you will be less likely to agree to anything she asks you to do, remembering that last time it got you nowhere. "I can never satisfy you. Nothing can make you happy!" You become distant and she becomes a "nag." This happens not because you are bad at relationships, not because you are incompatible, not because you are growing apart, but because you do not understand how conflict works.

— **One Final Illustration** —

My former wife and I were discussing the tax deduction of our youngest daughter. The divorce decree stated that this year was my turn to claim my youngest daughter on my tax return. Her mother wanted to contest this, asking me to give her the deduction this year. As was our usual practice, we agreed to meet and talk about it. The conversation went something like this:

Former wife: "You have not fulfilled the
mandates of the divorce decree and could be
in trouble with the courts."

Notice the past tense verbs. She began with a description of the past, a description of my failures. Not taking the bait to negotiate the past, I used my communication skills to keep the door of communication open and explore the past with her. This exploration turned into an explanation of my irresponsible nature that, of course, led to my failure to fulfill the mandates of the divorce decree. Instead of defending myself, I asked her: "Is there anything else?" And there was...more of the same.

Say I would have defended myself. What would I have gained?

"I did fulfill the decree mandates! I am not
irresponsible! You are the one who blows
everything out of proportion. You..."

Where am I going with all of this defensiveness: the truth? Let's say I convince her of "the truth." What have I gained? She still wants the tax deduction. We still have to make a decision together around who gets to apply the deduction this year. How well do you think our decision-making discussion would go after I convinced her she was completely wrong about me, about the divorce decree, about her understanding of the situation?

> *"You're wrong, I'm right! Now that that is*
> *all cleared up, let's decide who will get this*
> *year's tax deduction."*

All of this defensiveness gets me nothing. Don't negotiate the past. Get to the future.

> *"What are you asking me to do?"*

> *"I want you to give me this year's tax*
> *deduction."*

We have crossed the pivot point, out of the past and into the future. We may drop back into the past occasionally, but a good conflict resolver can get the conversation back to the future with respect and relative ease.

This is her "orange." The tax deduction "fixes" something for her. My job is to figure out what it is. I must do need exploration.

When I asked her,

> *"Why do you want the tax deduction?"*

she heard,

> *"Explain to me why you think you should get it!"*

This took us right back into the past. "I told you, you have not done what you were supposed to."

So I had to rephrase the question. "How will the tax deduction help you this year?" (Notice: "for what purpose?")

> *"It will make it so I will not have to pay as much tax this year!"*

I then narrowed to what I thought her need might be with an impact question.

> *"If you do not get the tax deduction this year what impact will it have on your life?"*

> *"It will severely hurt my budget."*

Now I test my conclusion that her need is, in fact, cash flow:

> *"So, if we could figure out a way not to negatively impact your cash flow this year, then could I keep this year's tax deduction?"*

> *"How do you plan to do that?"*

> *"What if I paid you the difference you*
> *would have to pay if you didn't get the tax*
> *deduction? I could write you a check for the*
> *difference and keep the tax deduction myself."*

> *"That could work."*

Many think the conflict is over and write the check, failing to address the bilateral nature of any commitment. I now ask the benefit question,

> *"If I do this, will you agree to not ask for any*
> *more money from me not already designated*
> *in the decree?"*

> *"Yes."*

> *"Then, calculate the difference and I will*
> *write you a check for that amount."*

Because I own my own business, the tax deduction is worth more to my bottom line than the amount on the check I would write to her for the difference. She got her need met, and I got the tax benefits I needed that year.

When I tell this story, some complain that I gave in and gave too much. I had the written court decree on my side. It stated this was my year to claim this deduction. I could have won this argument in court and not have had to pay her anything at all, but at what cost? "Winning" is not always a win. By behaving this way, I meet her need, I meet my need, and all without any damage to the relationship that might sabotage future negotiations.

— Conclusion —

Phase one of a conflict corresponds to the past. Explore the past, do not negotiate the past. I use my communication skills to explore the other person's understanding of what happened. The phase one question I typically ask is:

> *"What happened that caused you to be so upset?"*

Phase two of a conflict corresponds to the future. The future is where resolution lies, not in the past. I use my resolution skills to explore the needs of the other person, keeping my needs in mind as well. The phase two question I typically ask is:

> *"What is it you are asking me to do?"*

Phase three of a conflict corresponds to my commitment to a particular future. I want to commit to an action plan that will positively affect the emotional response created by the other person's perspective on my past action. That is, I want to commit to something that will produce an outcome that at least will not endanger my needs and at best meet both of our needs. The phase three question I typically ask is:

> *"What benefits will come from doing what is being asked of me?"*

There are two aspects to negotiating the future. The first is raising the pivot point question that gets us out of the past, into proposals for future action and application of need exploration skills. The second aspect is understanding the mutual benefits of any proposed future action plan for both parties and applying your negotiation skills.

> A great conflict resolver must master three skills.

Three skills are necessary for a great conflict resolver: communication skills, resolution skills and negotiation skills. Communication skills correspond to exploring the past and healthy venting, keeping the door of communication open. Remember, I cannot resolve a conflict with someone I am not talking to. Then, resolution and negotiation skills correspond to negotiating the future. Resolution skills get me across the threshold of the door my communication skills kept open, and negotiation skills navigate me to an action plan that produces bilateral benefits.

All this sounds pretty me- chanical here. There is noth- ing magical about these three phase questions. Learning these questions is the easy part. Listening for the three phases of a conflict is not that hard. Knowing when to ask what ques-

> Change the way you think about conflict. Conflict can be your friend.

tion, weaving your skills into the conversation in a way that understands conflict dynamics, is more difficult.

These skills take time to incorporate into daily living. What I am asking you to do is change the way you think about conflict. It is not the bad, evil thing you were taught to avoid at all cost. You must begin to understand that the cost of avoiding conflict is heftier than you were led to be- lieve. You lose so much when you try to live as though it is possible to eliminate conflict from your life. Conflict can be your friend. It can bring you so many positive things, if you will learn how conflict works and utilize a few effective skills to pull out its positive potential.

Practicing these skills has changed my life. I hope they bring you similar success.

— The Time to Fight Worksheet —

(Perform these tasks on a separate sheet of paper.)

1) Think about your last argument (either in a personal setting or in your professional setting).

    a. What was your "orange?"
    b. To what end were you "demanding" this?
    c. What impact would it have had in your life if you did not get this?
    d. What impact would it have had in your life if you did get this?

2) What to you think your need was?

3) List at least ten things that could be done to meet this need. Remember to put on the list your "demand."

4) Think about your last argument (either in a personal setting or in your professional setting).

    a. Where were you stuck in the past?
    b. What could you have said to explore the past (not negotiate it) by Summarizing or Paraphrasing the other person's point of view?
    c. What could you have asked to explore the past, by

Asking a Probing Question?

    d. What could you have said to explore the past, by Validating when you could?

    e. What could you have said to explore the past, by Identifying Emotions?

5) Remembering parts of your last argument, list any criticisms directed toward you.

6) Translate the Positive Request in each of the criticisms listed in #5.

7) Think about your last argument (either in a personal setting or in your professional setting).

    a. What proposal was being asked of you? What was their "orange?"

    b. Was their proposal a punishment?

    c. If so, write a question (without using the word "punishment") you could ask. Consider a question using the word "benefit" and one not using the word "benefit."

    d. Repeat their proposal to yourself and say: "That's one option."

    e. To what end were they "demanding" this?

    f. What impact would it have had in their life if they did not get this?

g. What impact would it have had in their life if
   they did get this?

8) What do you think their need was?

9) List at least ten things that could be done to meet
this need. Remember to put on the list their "demand" of
you.

10) Put a check next to the things you might have con-
sidered doing on the list of items under #9.

11) Put a check next to the things you might have con-
sidered accepting on the list of items under #3.

Personal Notes and Lessons Learned

About the Author

Dr. Richard Voyles, President of Conflict Resolution Academy, located in Smyrna Georgia, has a broad-based knowledge in the area of alternative dispute resolution techniques, mediation and leadership development. He travels internationally training people in the areas of prejudice reduction, cross-cultural communication, conflict management, management and leadership skills. As a Registered Neutral with the State of Georgia, he works with the court systems to mediate disputes for everything from Civil cases, Special Education, Elder Care, Divorce and Couples issues. With a background in peacekeeping and diversity, Dr. Voyles has served on the Board of Directors for the Interfaith Coalition of Atlanta, and as a Commissioner for the Georgia Commission on the Holocaust. He currently serves on the Board of Directors for the Georgia Association for Conflict Resolution. His credits include designing training programs for leadership, diversity and conflict management for both corporate and federal organizations. His most recent projects include Relationship Skills training and Church Conflict program design and implementation. He is a published author and a highly sought after speaker and coach across the United States.

Learn to Resolve Conflict
Studying with

Dr. Rick Voyles

Start Your Career as a
Conflict Resolution Professional

- Be a Professional Mediator
- Be a Conflict Management Specialist
- Learn to Negotiate like a Pro

For information on how to get started in the fast growing field of conflict resolution go to
www.DrRickV.com

For information on how to hire Dr. Rick Voyles. as a
Mediator, Executive Coach or Speaker go to
www.DrRickV.com